O'NIGHTS

O'NIGHTS

by Cecily Parks

ALICE JAMES BOOKS
FARMINGTON, MAINE

10 9 8 7 6 5 4 3 2

Alice James Books are published by Alice James Poetry Cooperative, Inc., an affiliate of the University of Maine at Farmington.

Alice James Books
114 Prescott Street
Farmington, ME 04938
www.alicejamesbooks.org

Library of Congress Cataloging-in-Publication Data

Parks, Cecily.
  [Poems. Selections]
  O'Nights / Cecily Parks.
    pages ; cm
  ISBN 978-1-938584-11-4 (softcover : acid-free paper)
  I. Title.
  PS3616.A7554A6 2015
  811'.6--dc23
                    2014030175

Alice James Books gratefully acknowledges support from individual donors, private foundations, the University of Maine at Farmington, and the National Endowment for the Arts.

ART WORKS.
arts.gov

Cover Art: Charles Ephraim Burchfield (1893-1967), "Dandelion Seed Heads and the Moon," circa 1961-65; watercolor, gouache, charcoal, white chalk, sgraffito, on lightly textured white wove paper faced on ¼ inch thick laminated gray cardboard, 56" x 39 5/8". Karen and Kevin Kennedy Collection, reproduced with permission of the Charles E. Burchfield Foundation.

Contents

*

Acknowledgments

I am grateful to the editors of the following journals in which these poems first appeared, sometimes with different titles and in different forms: *32 Poems, Another Chicago Magazine, Boog City, The Concord Saunterer: A Journal of Thoreau Studies, Gulf Coast, The Kenyon Review, KR Online, Love Among the Ruins, Memorious, The New Yorker, The Offending Adam, Orion, Oversound, Phantom Limb, Redivider, Tongue, Tupelo Quarterly, Virginia Quarterly Review, WE ARE SO HAPPY TO KNOW SOMETHING 2*, and *The Yale Review*.

"Speculation at the Mountaintop Observatory" also appeared on *Verse Daily*.

"Fieldfare," "The Hospital at the End of the Forest" (originally titled "Yucatan Nightjar"), and "Twelve-Wired Bird-of-Paradise" appeared in *Birdlands*, a poetry-and-print collaboration with the artist Ken Buhler, and also in *"This music crept by me upon the waters. . . ,"* a group exhibition at Lesley Heller Workspace in New York.

I am indebted to Karen and Kevin Kennedy, Julie Graham and Maria Friedrich, and the Charles E. Burchfield Foundation for generously helping me secure permission to use "Dandelion Seed Heads and the Moon" to accompany these poems, which are influenced and inspired by Burchfield's astonishing way of looking at the natural world.

Thank you to the MacDowell Colony, Constance Saltonstall Foundation for the Arts, Virginia Center for the Creative Arts, Texas State University, and Yaddo for the support that assisted the completion of this collection. Thank you to Thoreau Farm for the desk, window, and quiet spring day in the room where Thoreau was born.

I am grateful to many friends, writers, artists, and readers for responding to my work, especially Ken Buhler, Brian Burt, Jennifer Chang, Amy Clark, Nadia Colburn, Leigh Anne Couch, Carrie Doyle, Sari Edelstein, Erica Ehrenberg, Farnoosh Fathi, Geoffrey Hilsabeck, Rowena Kennedy-Epstein, Sally Wen Mao, Andrew Mockler, Lynne Potts, Joan Richardson, Nida Sophasarun, Jonathan Weinert, and Leslie Williams. To Carey Salerno, Alyssa Neptune, Nicole Wakefield, Julia Bouwsma, and everyone responsible for the wonder that is Alice James Books: thank you for taking such good care of this book. To my family: thank you always for your love and encouragement. Lastly, begrudgingly, I have to thank my husband's family medicine residency program for the solitude and writing time that it provided me when my husband worked long days and even longer nights. This book is for him.

For Nick

Nov. 6. ...I guessed at Goodwin's age on the 1st. He is hale and stout and looks younger than he is, and I took care to set him high enough. I guessed he was fifty-five, and he said that if he lived two or three months longer he would be fifty-six. He then guessed at my age, thought I was forty. He thought that Emerson was a very young-looking man for his age, "But," said he, "he has not been out o'nights as much as you have."

— *The Journal of Henry David Thoreau*

Hurricane Song

The pines dizzying for a hurricane, the wind
so hotly twirls their skirts and underskirts,
unnerves their pinecones, ratchets up and up
their branches into needle-spangled, needle-spraying
plumes. The white-running sunlight falls and tumbles
through the meadow, rattling the grass. The meadow
sweeps me up in its arms so that I lose track of east
and feel that little kidnapped thrill that comes with drastic
weather. O almost-wilderness, will the hurricane
hunt this far inland for our green juice? I guess
yes. The meadow guesses wet where it laps up
against the soft remnants of wall. The clouds guess wind
behind the swervy treetops. Blue jays vanish in the orchard's
green. A deer flips herself over and over, white tail-spark,
black hoof-sparks, brown wheel. The clouds
guess again: shadows blooming and wilting in the grass,
latticed branch-shadow mottling the road. The sound
of kisses increases through the forest, switchy sticks.
The forest has loved itself long enough to do this.
Is now when I should love myself into a safer place,
or is this the place where love makes me safe? I guess yes

and yes. Spastic gods, the grasshoppers manifest
on the margins of errant leaves and spring into bright
nothing. Where do they come from, where do they go?
The wild strawberries guess wind. The wind guesses wind.
The grass guesses grass, tossing all of us.

When I Was Thoreau at Night

I covered my head so as to better hide
from men and see the moon, with whom
I carried on a conversation that illuminated

like lantern-swing, iterating and reiterating trees.
I asked, *What is my wild original?*
The moon said, *You dream me.*

Underfoot, aromatic crush.
I said, *I marry you.* The moon said, *You cannot husband me.*
Overhead, darkness circuited through

its diamond guides. If I were lonely, I loved loneliness.
If I were hungry, I ate battered apples. One star said, *Pilgrim.*
One star said, *Peregrine.* Peregrine. The name

of the first English child born in the brackish
New World. How I envied him, crying into
the wilderness with a name meaning wanderer.

My name seemed tame. How I hoped the farmers
would not find me in this woods, wearing this dress.
I asked the stars, *Will you be my jewelry?*

The stars said, *Follow us*. They drew me deep
into the disheveled spruces to introduce me
to loss. My fields were ill. They weren't my fields.

My trees were being killed. They weren't my trees.
I was nervous that this natural world would see
that I was filthy-footed in silk, a woman

pretending to be the man
to trip a pyrotechnic grace. Oh yes,
I wanted the world to be wild again. I believed

I might hold weather in my hands
and mend it. The night was finite, or infinite.
Expending my expiring decadence in modern

thirst, I tempted biography to invent me.
Weird nun in the night garden, I dipped my face,
yes, my face, in every honeyed pond and could not drink.

The Swallow Dips Her Wings in Midnight Pools

My swallow-chasing on the boardwalk
distresses the swamp, each footfall

reverberating through the pilings
and into the bruise-hued water under.

I stop with the swallow
when she fills herself with rest

on the dead tree.
I run when she drops.

She dips her wings in her reflection
but I cannot. When I lean

my head-and-shoulder silhouette
over the railing, the unsettled swamp water

will not reflect it. Swamp, forgive me;
I want to touch what looks like me.

Postpastoral

I borrowed an axe
so heavy I had to drag it
through the woods.

Branches couldn't catch
the geese or the sliding sun
and the mud-streaked axe blade

and my mud-streaked dress
took on a violet sheen.
I would build a house

to be lonely in. Across
the pond a train grated
through trees. From the woods

came the voice of foxes' paws
in leaves. From the air
an owl voice pleading

with the moon.
I asked the trees for boards,
shingles, laths

before I swung the axe
to split a birch.
I only nicked it.

The tree began to weep.
I licked what it wept.
I would own the forest.

PALUSTRINE

Though sleep is a form of hunting,
it doesn't feed.

Against the alder tilts my lean-to
thatched with branches—a pile

of tree pieces propped over my sleeping bag
patterned with bees.

Half of my heart forages.
Half of my heart fumbles

for the zipper pull between the wings.
Cartridged in the surrounding brambles

are berries that I shouldn't eat.
I already ate them, did I say that?

Recklessly is how I kiss
my compass. Commuting through

this version of directionless excursion,
I thank untrustworthy fruits and low-slung moons

for slinking around my wild-willed bivouac
in this toxic garden. Shelters have

their own weather. Before mystery tilts
into fear, the marsh unloads its mist

for another place to bear.

AMPHIBIOUS

A red salamander
skirts the lowland pool.
Leaf muck

in a dark ring
shows how the pool
shrinks. I wade

and in a few hours
I wade again
not remembering

the information
my skin collected
when I was wetted

before. I'm forgetting
how to be a woman.
I look for other bodies.

My toes masquerade
as stones
in the river.

I leave my hand
in a ditch beside
the road

and ditchwater
lays purple-backed grass
over it.

BELL

Here gray birches lying down
with the silversmithing wind.

Here a fawn fiercely curled
against the smithereening spring.

Ears ringing, I belly up to my queendom
of nimblewill and bicycle chains,

grease slicking my hem the color of gravel
with no brook to gravel in. Belled

bicycle listing, I play the game
where the object is to keep falling.

My knees sing. Here birds nest
in the curved gravel road.

I confess: I doubted the presence
of the road and the breathing

of the stones
until I became intimate with them.

The Forest for the Trees

I believe it's all this pollen that dizzies me.
I chance and re-chance upon
the stalks of wild asparagus, the crimson
rhubarb, the fern splayed into
the cow road's muck.
Is it my eye or sundown pin-tucking the ravine?

I believe my panting
leaves wet blossoms
on the branches of this one tree.
Willing my mouth to press against elm
and ironwood, I have inklings of missing
but not of what I should miss.
Solitude is like this, a distance I walk toward
but never into.
Strings of spit testify to the bark I've kissed.

SILVICULTURE

Around a twitchy center
the willow branches
steer and swat me.

The rain equivocates,
wanting to rise as steam
before it falls as water

and extracts my promise
to be hotter after.
I promise to be hotter after.

I gather the willow's weepings
in my bare arms and press them
against my chest.

Out of all the places
I've worn this sleeveless dress
only the woods has been the place

for lust. What sadness
the willow knows
about domesticity

irrevocably taming me
I counter with a haze-day
dream: this rain is a home.

That lake is a room.
The minnows are windows
in my every wall.

How will I ever set fire
to the woods
if it continues to be as wet

as this? In the ankle-scraping
scrub-shrub, I test
the delirious trees.

A LANDSCAPE THAT ACCOMMODATES SPILL

This crooked morning

indexes every gray

in its quiver.

Bottom-feeding fog

in the toothsome hollow.

Wild olive tree

at the nape

of the sulky pond's neck.

The pond's lazy eye.

Is this my final

or penultimate pond?

To whom did I promise,

in a syrupy voice,

my stumbling in?

Thunder, then thunder.

The imminent rain's

spangling. I bobby-pin

my hair with the brightest

double-pronged pins.

I Have Set Fire to the Forest

I put on a dress to walk
in the seeping rain, believing
that if the willows are suddenly green

I might have something sudden happen
to me. I saunter impatiently.
The pond would insure against loneliness

but the rain distresses its surface
so much that I can't see
myself in it. All of my will-o'-the-wisps

drown then. Rain sleeks
down the fire-blackened trees. Whose
forgiveness are we (the pond, the

will-o'-the wisps, the forest and I) waiting
for? My dress snatches at my armpits
like a baby squirrel I might take back

to my cabin to nurse and coax

into companioning me. No. If I were

Thoreau, spring would make me want

to destroy something. So I become

the crocus ripping through the dirt, the screaming

forsythia. Silence my tinder.

I scream for a soul with a will

that huffs and puffs to fill the bud

in me with the syrup and stuffing I need

to bloom. Like the pussy willows

I know I'll bloom eventually

and when I do, people will want to touch me.

Aubade with Foxes

All night foxes ranged over the snow crust
barking raggedly. This morning

a warm rain softens the snow and dumbly
I watch my love sweep it off the windshield

and drive away. I'm in the road in little more
than underwear, suspended in the edgy bliss

of exhaust with two flights of stairs to climb.
In dens nearby the coiled foxes lick

their teeth and cover their eyes
with bushy, white-tipped tails. When I go

inside, my bare feet leave curved wet-marks
on the stairway's metal treads. A fox

will arc along a wall knowing the stone
won't hold her scent. When a fox runs in leaves

her sound is a rustle of leaves. No one is looking
or listening for me. Nearby a bell hits its notes.

Which version of heaven will feed me
until my love comes home? In one, I understand

what the foxes say. In the other, the foxes
find what they want and are quiet with it.

Morning Instructions for the Doctor's Wife

Accept the window
that gives you glass, the dawn
that gives you the maple branch
with a single bud, meadowlarks
singing where you can't see them.
Keep your black nightgown on,
more night than gown.
Wolves in the wallpaper.
Read an article about a man
who coughed blood. If you don't learn
who lives next door to you, you
can leave the curtains open
all the time. Only at certain times
can a body be sexual. The doe
that meets your gaze in the meadow
isn't sexual. When surgeons split
the coughing man's chest with a saw
and then his lung with a scalpel,
his body wasn't sexual.
At night the moon pulls
leaf buds out of the branch with silver
instruments. If you don't learn

how many bodies the doctor
places his fingers into
in a single day, yours will always
be the only. Inside
the coughing man's lung, the surgeons
found a fir tree. The dark interior
of a lung or a leaf bud, imagined
long enough, becomes a wilderness.
Your mind can do this
in the morning when you don't have
a body. Wilderness isn't paradise.

Wilderness

There is a hesitance to the trees.

There is unwillingness to the fence
even though it suggests spaces to crawl through

and crawl back through.

There is an entry
in an index on a page frail enough

for light to crawl into it.

I read by a goose. I read by a neck. I read by a lamp.
Blackflies litter the windowsill.

There is a house with an unpredictable staircase,

meager caulking, drafts.
The apertures consent to the cold

that consents to the rain

      that consents to the light
that consents to the upsweep of the branch
when what rests on it consents to the blank

      above it. There is a branch
certainly. The rest is the woodpile's reverie:

split kindling conjoining, quarters healing into halves, halves

      into wholes, wholes into deadfall, deadfall into trees
as the chopping block rolls

toward the ferns most shaped like forgiveness.

THE INTROSPECTIVE VOCABULARY

I wear a furtive when I climb up the hill
to deliver the first of the.

Of all of them, the first is the most,
written without hindsight. My blessings

count themselves thusly: if sound
is the prerequisite for searching, if being wary

is the prerequisite for laying down with,
if there is something worth facing east for,

then. Extending a single thought has something
to do with the half-shut and the fireplace soot

filling pails beside a fire. To take my time
coming to (in spite of arrowing triangulation

and every backstory orbiting a thorn) is tricky.
My believing keeps me believing.

An inglenook holds two secrets, one for
each of. My wisteria leads entirely to wisteria.

The Last Garden

The shadows grow deep enough
to wash my hands in them

in this last garden
where the statuary prepares

for ruin. I practice the listening
that stains the interlocutor like grass.

I practice grass.
The stone nymph leans

into the leanest wash of light
as if it held the remedy for debility and lichen

and all that algae in the fountain
beneath her feet. The carp creep up

out of the opaque to inhabit my silhouette
and each orange rotation

is a thought asking me to think it.
I think my love of lonesomeness

bewilders my love. I rove
as if I knew no chase more earnest

than that of rust
running over the trellis.

THE ORNITHOLOGY LAB AT NIGHT

An indigo ex-goddess
to roost in my ribs
and warn my heart of waylaying:

the concept breaks
and beautifully enters me.
My own canary, my own mine.

I picked the ornithology lab lock
as if it were a box's last
match. Would that it

were so. Eyeless in this arsenic
dark, I ransack floor-to-ceiling drawers
by index finger,

pushing against
irrevocably folded wings.
Among the feathered topographies

the spilling air
knew, nothing feels
indigo bunting blue.

Among the ankle-labeled
specimens, I worry
I will not find her. This blindness

feels familiar. I've been told
she is a lake
the size of a barrette, but duller than

her brother. All
the females are,
I whisper. I am the loudest animal here.

PILGRIM

The shadows practice night
along the river. I practice being a pilgrim.
I sew the button that will stop
my coat pocket from going crazy
in the wind. I run out
into the keeling grass so I can come back
wind-slapped and swooning
like woodsmoke. I'm hungry for November
to let me eat Thanksgiving dinner
at a long table where I sit next to my
meant-to-be and smooth my napkin.
Then I'm going to tell him how I lived
in the wild: I ran out of electricity
one autumn and camped outside,
sleeping by a stump whose rot
coincided with my idea of discipline.
November that year produced gaudy
squashes as long as infants, bulbous
and bruised from growing out of the stalk
and glowy flower. I talked
to the squashes. When I ran out

of conversation, I came inside and made amends

with my home, my socks, the length

of autumn. I doubted the winter

so fiercely that my electricity stayed lost.

I was going to practice being a pilgrim forever.

I was going to worship my head lamp

until its battery ran out. Then I thought better.

Now I think best. Inside this evening's

worth of destiny, November practices

its vagueness in the long grass

along the trail that leads me

to the November I invent for my love.

I run to coincide with the disappearing

light. I bring my pocket along.

LOVE POEM

I run with my mouth open. I open my mouth to breathe

into yours. On a whim

the Queen Anne's lace offers the roadside a galaxy.

I run. You take care of my breath.

You take care of it again.

Is this trust

or a consequence of summer's washes and concoctions?

Like one admonished for not darkening enough

of my nights, I ask further into the inflorescent

quiet. Once a woods, always a woods.

Sheet of mist on the unmade bed.

The sky begins at my mouth: star, moon, meteoric truck.

I find the wind. You find my west.

The contours of the pasture

repeat the contours of animals who wake

in the promise of grass.

I love exhaustion. I love it again.

Twelve-Wired Bird-of-Paradise

The peach that drops from the tree is speckled with blue as if it had been dimpled by the sky. We eat the motes of sky that the peach gives us.

We're still in paradise but don't know it.

We know: the trail through the woods studded with emerald and amethyst toadstools, the creek pitching gray over the stone that means to break it, the moss softening the rocks, the moss softening the stump, the green pond snug in the sedges, the reeds snug in the pond, the wind compelling the clouds, the clouds compelling the rain, the light ricocheting through the thunderstorm, the lantern faltering in the wind, the light

leading us homeward through the stammering rain that pine boughs hold and release after the rain.

Over and over, we describe the intricacy of transport that brought us here. It begins with the wish to be small enough to fit in each other's mouths, to be the taste of wind that leaps off the river, to be the taste of two currents braiding.

A bird named does not exist for us in its name, just as we don't know what the seed is if we don't know if it will let itself be pressed in our palm's deepest crease and warmed there.

The tree fills itself with peaches and in doing so, fills itself with shadows. We pluck a peach—subtracting a shadow from the branches and leaves—and eat it.

We make a fist around the seed.

Then we are inextricable, one taste, one shadow. We travel north along the river that weights the wind with water and then further north along the ocean that the river fills. We come to rest on the top floor of a peach-colored house surrounded by leaves.

We're afraid we'll die before we've loved each other long enough. There is no end

to long enough. This is paradise.

We open the fist with the seed in it. The birds here are brown and delight in bathing in the dust. The first one that touches us, we'll name.

Snow Song

When the wind
lifts crescents of snow
from bare branches

we remember leaves.
When the frozen pond
shifts and cracks

as the ice contracts
we remember oars
that clunked and spun

diving through dots
of light. We ask the snow
to be wool for us.

Aubade with Bicycle

Seven a.m. in December in the middle of the street
I buckle my bike helmet and

hearing a glassy tapping look up at my love
framed in a window the size of a door as if he might step out

onto the spindly branch of the maple and balance there.
He blows me a kiss

and I want to rush back into the house
up two flights of stairs and into his arms our bed

but this is the time of day we leave each other. The wind blows open
the spaces between the maple branches

the parked cars almost shiver in the gusts
and I set my bicycle licking

down the wet black street past the yellow house the purple house
the Christmas lights fruiting in the bushes

past the playground with its crowd
of leaves around the merry-go-round.

It rained in the night: the grass and mud ran
into the street and by the time

I reach the park flecks of mud have confettied
my shins my thighs. The puddles count the clouds.

The grass rises into a hill against a gray-blue sky
that unwraps itself to reveal another bluer sky.

A man in the field throws a yellow ball.
There is a silvery trail through the grass where his dog gives chase

and I let the bike go
down the hill past the matted barley-colored grasses

beyond which the marsh opens its little wet mouths
and my love must by now

be inside his car driving to work and so cannot feel this wind
blowing me back with such insistence that I wonder if

my bike makes any progress east as I seem to be taking forever
to slide by these slumped rows of cut Christmas trees that wait

for the nursery to open, for someone with gloved hands
to run those hands over them, take a deep breath

and say this is the one I want.

THE WINTER OF
AMATEUR CARDIOLOGY

At this old desk of orange wood striated by dark wavy lines, I think of electrocardiograms, heartbeats shimmying under my palms in a white room in winter. A window to my right, gray sky, twitchy bare branches. In the green of summer, a window full of maple leaves, I liked to think that I lived in a tree. Now hot water circulates to the silver radiator, knocks and wetly hisses. A painting hangs above the desk, to the left. To look at it, I lift and turn my head so my chin is over my heart. The radiator knocks. In the painting, a girl in a white dress followed by a white dog walks beside a pond. The dog is in mid-stride, one front paw a pendulum. Where I live, there is a pond where the bankside winter grasses seethe in the wind as I run past them. A red screech owl with a heart-shaped face and white-flecked wings lives in a tree there. The owl's feathers match the pattern of tree bark. The owl can resemble a broken branch, its call a whinny or trill. I've never seen it. I've seen the elderly bird watchers at dusk, whispering, the black wings of their binoculars over their hearts.

Skylight

While I run around the winter pond
you are already gathering the morning
in your quadrangular eye and making

a blue-and-white thought of it. Is it you
or the pond that I contemplate best?
The pond I run beside is soft and wet

when like sleep from an eye
the mist has been wiped from it.
I would like to wade, trap the clouds

in my pond-wet hands and swallow them.
Skylight, if you could see me you would know
that I know the hunger—your hunger—

to have the sky inside you. The eye—
my eye—feels the sad contrast
between your composition of slow clouds

and this spongy ground sucking my feet.
If you could see me running you would know
the wind scours my face and bruises the pond

but not the bankside panes of ice.
How can I love weather and a window too?
Winter love is the love of blemishes
and glass is what my panting blooms against.

Sinus Infection

Beneath my right eye
behind my hot cheek
back inside my skull

a pack of black
wolves howls.
The man across from me

in the library
white hair windswept
by thinking

might hear it—he looks
into a distance
that might include us

me him the wolves
who fall on furred shoulders flanks
rise and lunge

again starving for
moon woods ridge
the calves' shadows

in a meadow now
greenly unfolding
in the man's mind or

so I hope
because the wolves have
such tremendous paws

that I can only think
of extinction how badly
I want to own

the kind of gun
that kills them.
They lunge fangs-first

they gnaw at my cheekbone
they twist.
My right ear rings.

Dancing with the Doctor

If I,—
when you are
sleeping
and the landlady downstairs
her ashy dog
are sleeping
and the train that brought me home
is a wolf-black breath
breathing back
into coarse marshlands
along the coast,—
if I in our dining room
dressless
dance, wheezily
singing so not even
our infestation of moths
can hear: *I will never be daughter*
of the maple tree! I will never be
sister of the leaf!
If I admire
my hairless shins

and the purple gloss

of my polished fingernails running

over them in the light

cast by the street's mechanical

moon,—who shall say I am not

the woman

who says with her mouth

at your neck:

Love, when I told you

my wilderness was almost

wild, it meant

I hadn't loved a man

like a man yet.

Bell

This newness of snow. This boot-ringing
as the snow warms in the sun to crush. These holes
we wind around the witnessing pines. This
violation of white. This slowness of moose.
This counting of steps. This counting of scars
in the bark: the warty burl bulging low
on the trunk, the black scratchings left
by a bear learning to climb. This counting
of sleeps between this country and the next country
we call home. These branches shucking off
the statuesque in avalanches of needles and ice.
This progress, as in the wind-scalloped snow meadow
pretending to be moon. This love that sets us scrambling
over the map's last ridge, our red hoods bright
in shrunken sky. This metallic weather in which we
are the ore. This alder. These crimson-tipped willows
reverberating next to a river of turquoise ice. This
following the deep tracks of one coyote stepping
where another has stepped. This wilderness
that we trespass, burning like berries in the juniper
and becoming the air in the belfry.

Fieldfare

Field wing. Field sky.
Field fall. Field flung.

Field seed. Field sung.
Field fog. Field guess.

Field god. Field ghost.
Field line. Field swerve.

Field bone. Field nerve.
Field greed. Field sprawl.

Field weight. Field wall.
Field hay. Field stem.

Field drought. Field flame.
Field ash. Field awe.

Field myth. Field law.
Field paw. Field tail.

Field feet. Field trail.
Field pod. Field burst.

Field blades. Field thirst.
Field will. Field would.

Field hands. Field hold.
Field breath. Field pulse.

CONVERSATION BETWEEN FOX AND FIELD

Fox: Light as
moths, I leave

a trace of
arcs across.

Field: I give
chase until

the brambles,
woods, or fence.

ALICE JAMES

Am illnesses
of Alice and Alice's
Alice and as all
things Alice —
part Ah! part
opaque catechism
part ever
since the second
collapse — I have
passed through
every unbraidable
fiber not
as fiat
but as these
long pauses
shrieking for anchorage
where water
eloquently converts
the nervous succulent
to an impromptu
religion of green.

Girls Ride Shotgun in the Ice Cream Truck

They sing along to the jingle they know by heart, by shin, by skin. Waking is to happiness as the trash can is to raccoons and then some. Without pockets, they plumb the freezer for what fills the yellowing billows their hand-me-down aprons make—rocket ship popsicles, varieties of sprinkles, sugar cones on the verge of brittle. What melts makes them run, because if the changing of states isn't the universe's promise of a love abundant as a spider plant, it might be something better. Once dogged, the mundane refrains from their bare heels. Their paths give and give. It's the day before the longest day of the year, it's Indian summer, it's their birthday, it's snowing and they've never heard of winter.

SPECULATION AT THE
MOUNTAINTOP OBSERVATORY

I rehearse my rangy faith

in prospects

lying face down,

chin rocking on the lawn

and corner-eyeing the night.

From this vantage

the June grass spikelets

serrate the sky as if

incision were the next

transaction and heaven's spill

the next. The observatory

slathered in glue then silver

glitter. Carried away

by heretic astronomy,

my looking atomizes and flings

farther. The neglected

telescope rattles its moonfaced

lenses. The pathos

of the fixed point

is a derivative based on return,

but I would rather fall

again. I would rather

a ceiling strung with pinfire,
caving in. The asthmatic
engine of wonder still turns
me over. I spin.

HESPERIS MATRONALIS

A dandelion gleams
in the grass. I could smear it
against my neck

and brighten my throat.
I could sour my mouth
eating its jagged leaves, suck

the meat off sparrow bones
if I knew how to trap a bird
and open it.

Some nights I beg the moon
to swerve and hit me.
I think it would feel

like a blessing, my dress
a window to a gleaming body,
my body bent

under the weight of being
good.

After the dark mass
of sparrows shoves off
the plumed grasses, the stalks

sway. When birds circle,
are they waiting for the grasses
to be still

so they can touch them
again, or are they waiting
for the grasses to be good?

I try to turn
my mind to what I know,
like the grasses

which are called nimblewill.
Or this flowering weed,
mother-of-the-evening,

petals violet-blue as light
inside a drawer.

I know the field can be
a companion
but not my daughter.

I know grasses seem
to darken where they rub
against each other.

If the grass could wait, what
would it wait for?

BLUE OAT GRASS EPITHALAMIUM

Before we knew each other, blue oat grass
grew all around us, filling with soft spears
the spaces between our fingers, between

our ribs and outflung arms. The grass gently
separated our legs. We lived like this.
In the blue-blade woods we made by resting

on our backs in the meadow, we echoed
the dwarf blue spruce and the blue juniper.
We were too tired to look for anything

but the ceremonies of ebullient
clouds. Had one of us turned to find the other
lying there in grass, breathing deep enough

to grow a field in the lung, then the clouds
might have married us in a white riot.
Because we didn't look for each other,

the stones crept up out of the dry phantom
of a river to bury us. We were
tired. We let them. In the river's blue dream,

loneliness flooded us with honey
and slush, a current mineral-thick with what
it had stripped from the mountains. Every

afternoon an uprising of ravens.
A wolf was a day of the year. The stones
promised to be our weather until

we found the love that would grant more than afterlife:
it would require us to live. We lived
like this: we ate the stones, wetting them

with our mouths so they would raft down our throats
without disturbing the fields in our lungs.
Our breathing was the blue oat grass breathing

through us with rasp enough to wake the river
from its dream of water. Like water,
the grass pushed blue against the undersides

of the stones and split them. We were made
of meadow and will. With the strength we'd saved for
eternity, we turned to face each other.
Blue oat grass lay down between us to let us look.

The Hospital at the End of the Forest

The roosters describe all

candlelit night the luck that hoards itself

in baskets of yellow apples and in

the murky foliage of the hospital arbor under

which the mothers gaze through the pane

love glazes between the body and the body

in sickness their breathing a prescription

for the lungs leafing inside the newborn bodies

that cry because of crying

they can be certain as certain as the green ridge

that fires a sunrise in whose light

I love no one harder than the doctor

beside me and though I believe in medicine and in

the unstructured sweetness

of the summer tanagers I most believe

that he and I went through separate

successions of illnesses and orchards to alight

at this hospital at forest-end where mothers

say nothing under the riffling ceiling

of vines wafting their leafing

through the library where a textbook

of extraordinary diseases scares me past

speculation into the inevitable suspicion

that when my body smashes itself to smithereens

and what mind remains bears witness

to the path we broke through our particular trees

there will be confusions

of wings and applelight and though

I'll not know then what my body moves toward

I'll know our bodies were here now

touching sometimes

in the evenings the roosters make known.

Notes

"When I Was Thoreau at Night"

The phrase "wild original" comes from Thoreau's essay "Wild Apples." He writes: "Pliny, adopting the distinction of Theophrastus, says, 'Of trees there are some which are altogether wild, some more civilized.' Theophrastus includes the apple among the last; and, indeed, it is in this sense the most civilized of all trees. It is as harmless as a dove, as beautiful as a rose, and as valuable as flocks and herds. It has been longer cultivated than any other, and so is more humanized; and who knows but, like the dog, it will at length be no longer traceable to its wild original?"

Peregrine White was born to William and Susanna White aboard the Mayflower while it was docked in Provincetown Harbor. The name Peregrine can mean wanderer, traveler, or stranger.

"The Swallow Dips Her Wings in Midnight Pools"

The title comes from a line in Virginia Woolf's *The Waves*. The image of a dipping swallow repeats throughout those passages written from Rhoda's point of view.

"I Have Set Fire to the Forest"

Thoreau accidentally set fire to hundreds of acres of woods near Walden Pond. In his journal he writes: "It was a glorious spectacle, and I was the only one there to enjoy it. The fire now reached the base of the cliff and raced up its sides. The squirrels ran before it in blind haste, and three pigeons dashed into the midst of the smoke. The flames flashed up the pines to their tops, as if they were powder…"

"Aubade with Foxes"

"Sometimes I heard the foxes as they ranged over the snow crust, in moonlight nights, in search of partridge or other game, barking raggedly and demoniacally like forest dogs, as if laboring with some anxiety, or seeking expression, struggling for light and to be dogs outright and run freely in the streets; for if we take the ages into our account, may there not be a civilization going on among brutes as well as men?" —Henry David Thoreau, *Walden*

"Wilderness"

"'Wilderness' has a deceptive concreteness at first glance. The

difficulty is that while the word is a noun it acts like an adjective. There is no specific material object that is wilderness. The term designates a quality (as the '-ness' suggests) that produces a certain mood or feeling in a given individual and, as a consequence, may be assigned by that person to a specific place. Because of this subjectivity a universally acceptable definition of wilderness is elusive."
—Roderick Frazier Nash, *Wilderness and the American Mind*

"The Introspective Vocabulary"

"This is all I have to say about the emotions. If one should seek to name each particular one of them which the human heart is the seat, it is plain that the limit to their number would lie in the introspective vocabulary of the seeker..."—William James, *The Principles of Psychology, vol 2*

"Dancing with the Doctor"

This poem owes much to William Carlos Williams's poem "Danse Russe."

"Alice James"

This poem, which borrows language from Jean Strouse's *Alice James: A Biography*, could not have been written had I not read Jennifer Chang's poem "Dorothy Wordsworth."

"*Hesperis matronalis*"

Christine Elfman's series of photographs *Hesperis matronalis : mother of the evening* was one of the forces guiding this poem. The flower *Hesperis matronalis* has many names, including dame's rocket, damask violet, dame's violet, dames-wort, dame's gilliflower, night-scented gilliflower, sweet rocket, and mother-of-the-evening. It releases its fragrance at night.

Carrie Patterson

Cecily Parks is the author of the chapbook
Cold Work, winner of the Poetry Society of
America/New York Chapbook Fellowship,
and the collection *Field Folly Snow*, which
was a finalist for the Norma Farber First
Book Award. Her poems have appeared in
*Kenyon Review, Orion, The New Yorker,
The Yale Review*, and elsewhere. She teaches
at Texas State University and lives in Austin,
Texas.

Recent Titles from Alice James Books

Yearling, Lo Kwa Mei-en

Sand Opera, Philip Metres

Devil, Dear, Mary Ann McFadden

Eros Is More, Juan Antonio González Iglesias,
Translated by Curtis Bauer

Mad Honey Symposium, Sally Wen Mao

Split, Cathy Linh Che

Money Money Money | Water Water Water, Jane Mead

Orphan, Jan Heller Levi

Hum, Jamaal May

Viral, Suzanne Parker

We Come Elemental, Tamiko Beyer

Obscenely Yours, Angelo Nikolopoulos

Mezzanines, Matthew Olzmann

Lit from Inside: 40 Years of Poetry from Alice James Books, Edited by
Anne Marie Macari and Carey Salerno

Black Crow Dress, Roxane Beth Johnson

Dark Elderberry Branch: Poems of Marina Tsvetaeva, A Reading by
Ilya Kaminsky and Jean Valentine

Tantivy, Donald Revell

Murder Ballad, Jane Springer

Sudden Dog, Matthew Pennock

Alice James Books has been publishing poetry since 1973. The press was founded in Boston, Massachusetts as a cooperative wherein authors performed the day-to-day undertakings of the press. This collaborative element remains viable even today, as authors who publish with the press are also invited to become members of the editorial board and participate in editorial decisions at the press. The editorial board selects manuscripts for publication via the press's annual, national competition, the Alice James Award. Alice James Books seeks to support women writers and was named for Alice James, sister to William and Henry, whose extraordinary gift for writing went unrecognized during her lifetime.

Designed by Pamela A. Consolazio
LITTLE FROG DESIGNS